RICH[ARD WAGNER]

PARSIFAL

Prelude to the Sacred Drama
Vorspiel zum Bühnenweihfestspiel
WWV 111

Edited by/Herausgegeben von
Egon Voss

Ernst Eulenburg Ltd

London · Mainz · Madrid · New York · Paris · Prague · Tokyo · Toronto · Zürich

CONTENTS

Preface III

Vorwort VI

Parsifal. Prelude 1

Reprinted from Richard Wagner: Sämtliche Werke
Volume 14/I by permission of Schott Music GmbH & Co. KG

© 2019 Ernst Eulenburg & Co GmbH, Mainz
for Europe excluding the British Isles
Ernst Eulenburg Ltd, London
for all other countries

Ernst Eulenburg Ltd
48 Great Marlborough Street
London W1F 7BB

PREFACE

Wagner's first closer look at the *Parsifal* material dates back to the period of his studies for the *Lohengrin* libretto, for Lohengrin is known, according to legend, to be Parsifal's son. Wagner therefore read Wolfram von Eschenbach's epic *Parzival* during the summer of 1845.[1] That he was already contemplating the subject matter as a model for a stage work, as has repeatedly been claimed, cannot be substantiated.

In 1857, Wagner considered having Parsifal, who was in search of the Grail, appear at Tristan's sickbed in the 3rd act of *Tristan und Isolde*,[2] even notating a melody for this.[3] After that, the topic seems to have been ever on his mind. The first ideas can be found in his letters of 1858-1860 to Mathilde Wesendonck, the muse of *Tristan*.[4] Following in the summer of 1865 was the inscription of the first prose draft, at the insistence of Wagner's patron King Ludwig II of Bavaria.[5] The plan was to première the work in Munich in 1872.[6] Nothing, however, came of that. To be completed and performed first of all were *Die Meistersinger von Nürnberg* and *Der Ring des Nibelungen*, all of this taking place up to 1876. Only then could Wagner tackle *Parsifal*, starting in February 1877.

The compositional process now proceeded along the same pattern as that of nearly all of Wagner's other stage works. Ensuing after a prose draft, the second in this case,[7] was the libretto from which a fair copy was immediately prepared as the model for printing.[8] Thereafter, Wagner began the composing, initially in the form of a pencilled continuity sketch (com-positional sketch), but accompanied from the outset, with a time lag, by a second, more detailed inked sketch (orchestral sketch). Only after concluding this work (in April 1879) did Wagner move on to the score, which was completed at the beginning of 1882.[9] The work's first performance took place on 26 July 1882 in the Bayreuth Festival Hall.

During work on the text Wagner changed the title of the work and the name of the protagonist to *Parsifal*, because he made the assumption – though erroneous – that "Fal-par-si", the syllabic conversion of Par-si-fal, meant "pure fool" in Arabic.[10]

Wagner no longer saw his stage works as operas in the traditional sense, and to characterise their distinctiveness, he provided them with unusual subtitles. Thus, *Der Ring des Nibelungen* is called "A Stage Festival [*Bühnenfestspiel*]" and *Parsifal*, "A Stage-Consecrating Festival [*Bühnenweihfestspiel*]". Wagner explained what is meant by this name in his report on the first performance, *Das Bühnenweihfestspiel in Bayreuth 1882* [The Stage-Consecrating Festival in Bayreuth in 1882].[11] The word "Weihe" in the title is not to be understood as primarily religious, but is aimed rather at the originally cultic, ceremonially ritualistic sense of theatre. Therefore, for the execution of the music it is wrong to choose tempi that are, in principle, slow and "solemn".

The Prelude was orchestrated in advance because Wagner wanted to have it performed for his wife Cosima on her birthday, 25 December 1878. For this, he engaged the Meiningen Hofkapelle [court orchestra] to play

---

[1] *Richard Wagner, Sämtliche Werke,* vol. 30, *Dokumente zur Entstehung und ersten Aufführung des Bühnenweih-festspiels Parsifal,* eds. Martin Geck and Egon Voss (Mainz, 1970), 11, Document 1.
[2] Ibid., 12, Documents 4-5.
[3] Ibid., 13, Document 8.
[4] Ibid., 13-17, Documents 9-13.
[5] Ibid., 68-77.
[6] Ibid., 17, Document 16.
[7] Ibid., 77-87.
[8] Ibid., 87-134.

[9] Cf. *Wagner-Werk-Verzeichnis* (Mainz, 1986), 544f. (WWV 111 MUSIK II, III, VI).
[10] Verses 689-691: I named you, pure fool, "Fal parsi", – You, pure fool: "Parsifal". (Verse numbering from: *Richard Wagner, Parsifal. Ein Bühnenweihfestspiel. Textbuch mit Varianten der Partitur,* ed. Egon Voss (Stuttgart, 2005).
[11] Wagner, *Sämtliche Werke* (see fn. 1), 63-67, Document 241.

the piece under his direction in the Haus Wahn-fried.[12] The manuscript of this first version of the Prelude, which was to be replaced by a second version in the score of the whole work, is extant and appears in print for the first time in the volume 21 supplement to the edition *Richard Wagner, Sämtliche Werke.* Coming from there is also the concert closing imparted here.

Wagner himself explained the Prelude in a text that he wrote on the occasion of performing it for Ludwig II of Bavaria on 12 November 1880:[13]

Prelude to Parsifal.
Love – Faith – : Hope?
First theme: "Love".
    "Accept my body, accept my blood, for the sake of our love!"
    (repeated by hovering angel voices.)
    "Accept my blood, accept my body, that you may remember mine!"
    (repeated again, hovering.)
Second theme: "Faith".
    Promise of salvation through faith. – Faith declares itself firmly and vigorously, intensifying, unshakeable even in suffering. – Faith, from the tenderest heights – as on the white dove's plumage, answers the renewed promise, the breast descending ever wider and fuller, engaging the human heart, the world, fulfilling all nature with the most powerful force, – then gazing up again towards the heavenly ether as gently soothed. –

    There, once more, out of the shudders of loneliness trembles the lament of loving compassion: fear, the holy anguish of the Mount of Olives, the divine suffering of Golgotha, – the body blanches, the blood escapes, and now burns with heavenly bliss in the chalice, living and suffering above all else is the joy of salvation's grace by the outpouring of love. – For him, who, – terrible remorse in his heart – had to immerse himself in the divine punitive sight of the glowing Grail, for Amfortas, the sinful guardian of the sanctuary, we are prepared: will his gnawing soul suffering become redemption? – Once again we hear the promise, and – hope!

"Love – Faith – Hope" is obviously an allusion to I Corinthians 13:13, St. Paul's letter to the Corinthians from the New Testament, which reads (King James Version): 'And now abideth faith, hope, charity [love], these three; but the greatest of these is charity.'

With respect to the musical themes, the Prelude does not mirror the whole plot. It conveys only the world of the Grail. At the start, the melody is heard in "Nehmet hin meinen Leib..." (A-flat major) and is repeated, shifted to C minor, in "Nehmet hin mein Blut..." The "Liebesmahl-Spruch [love-feast saying]", as Hans von Wolzogen, Wagner's Adlatus, called the theme,[14] is followed in bar 39 by the "Grail motif",[15] in which Wagner quotes the so-called Dresden Amen that he had previously already used in both *Liebesverbot* and *Tannhäuser* to indicate the Catholic-ecclesiastical sphere. Here, though, he took over the version that Felix Mendelssohn Bartholdy had given the theme in his fifth symphony, the so-called Reformation Symphony, which Wagner had heard in Bayreuth on 8 February 1876.[16] Perhaps he was of the opinion that Mendelssohn, for whom he had great respect, despite all anti-Semitism, had used the authentic version.

The "Faith" theme comes along as the third theme in bar 44.[17] No other themes are exposed, rather, Wagner gainsays the whole Prelude with the three themes mentioned and the motives derived from them. This means that the counter-world of the Grail, the magician Klingsor with his erotic flower girls and the

[12] *Cosima Wagner, Die Tagebücher*, eds. Martin Gregor Dellin and Dietrich Mack (München/Zürich, 1977), vol. 2, 270f.
[13] *König Ludwig II. und Richard Wagner. Briefwechsel*, edited by Otto Strobel (Karlsruhe, 1936), vol. III, 186f.

[14] *Hans von Wolzogen, Thematischer Leitfaden durch die Musik des Parsifal* (Leipzig, no year), 17.
[15] Ibid., 18.
[16] *Cosima Wagner, Tagebücher* (see fn. 12), 969.
[17] *Wolzogen, Leitfaden* (see fn. 14), 19.

temptress Kundry remain musically excluded. The Prelude includes nothing of the plot's dramatic conflicts.

The Prelude's opening proses a problem for the performers. Traditionally, the string instruments in bars 1-36 (except for the contrabasses) play, using mutes. But there is no direct evidence for this, either in Wagner's own autographs, in the Bayreuth performance score of 1882 or in the first edition of the Prelude. The directive first shows up in the score edition of the whole work, published after Wagner's death. It most likely goes back to a suggestion by the *Parsifal* conductor Hermann Levi, to which Wagner is said to have agreed. Nothing more precise can be said about that. But perhaps it is based on a misunderstanding, for triggering Levi's suggestion was probably the following: The Prelude's bars 6-19 and 25-38 correspond to bars 1445-1458 and 1464-1469, respectively, of the Grail scene in the 1st act. Stipulated there are mutes, though not in the Prelude, which is why Levi may have recommended an approximation that Wagner could have granted. The extension of the mute provision to bars 1-6 and 20-25 would then – possibly – be regarded as an error.[18]

The music text follows the Edition Eulenburg No. 8058, revised for the complete edition *Richard Wagner, Sämtliche Werke*, vol. 14, I, *Parsifal* WWV 111, eds. Egon Voss and Martin Geck (Mainz, 1972). The accompanying Critical Report can be found in vol. 14, III (Mainz, 1973), 157ff.

Egon Voss
Translation: Margit L. McCorkle

---

[18] Cf. on this topic: Stephan Mösch, *Weihe, Werkstatt, Wirklichkeit. „Parsifal" in Bayreuth 1882-1933* (Kassel, 2009), 147, 238. – Egon Voss, *Parsifal-Probleme. Besonderheiten der Bayreuther Aufführungen 1882 und ihre Folgen*, in: *wagnerspectrum* 12, volume 1/2016, 83-87.

VORWORT

Wagners erste nähere Beschäftigung mit dem Parzival-Stoff fällt in die Zeit seiner Studien zum Textbuch des *Lohengrin*; denn der Sage nach ist dieser bekanntlich der Sohn Parzivals. Wagner las daher im Sommer 1845 Wolfram von Eschenbachs Epos *Parzival*.[1] Dass er den Stoff schon zu dieser Zeit als Vorlage für ein Bühnenwerk ins Auge gefasst habe, wie immer wieder behauptet wird, lässt sich nicht beweisen.

Im Jahre 1857 erwog Wagner, den nach dem Gral suchenden Parzival im 3. Akt von *Tristan und Isolde*, an Tristans Krankenlager, auftreten zu lassen.[2] Er notierte dazu sogar eine Melodie.[3] Danach scheint ihn der Stoff nicht mehr losgelassen zu haben. Die ersten Gedanken finden sich in Briefen an Mathilde Wesendonck, die Muse des *Tristan*, aus den Jahren 1858-1860.[4] Es folgte im Sommer 1865, auf Drängen von Wagners Mäzen König Ludwig II. von Bayern, die Niederschrift des ersten Prosaentwurfs.[5] Geplant war, das Werk 1872 in München zur ersten Aufführung zu bringen.[6] Doch daraus wurde nichts. Zunächst waren *Die Meistersinger von Nürnberg* und *Der Ring des Nibelungen* zu vollenden und aufzuführen, was sich bis zum Jahr 1876 hinzog. Erst danach befasste sich Wagner erneut mit dem Parzival, beginnend im Februar 1877.

Der Schaffensprozess verlief nun nach dem Muster, nach dem fast alle Bühnenwerke Wagners geschaffen wurden. Auf einen Prosaentwurf – in diesem Falle der zweite[7] – folgte das Textbuch, von dem sogleich eine Reinschrift als Vorlage für den Druck angefertigt wurde.[8]

Danach begann Wagner mit der Komposition, zunächst in Gestalt einer umrisshaften Skizze in Bleistift (Kompositionsskizze), die aber von Beginn an, zeitversetzt, von einer zweiten ausführlicheren Skizze in Tinte (Orchesterskizze) begleitet wurde. Erst nach Abschluss dieser Arbeiten (April 1879) ging Wagner an die Partitur, die Anfang 1882 fertiggestellt wurde.[9] Die erste Aufführung des Werks fand am 26. Juli 1882 im Bayreuther Festspielhaus statt.

Während der Arbeit am Text änderte Wagner den Titel des Werks und den Namen des Protagonisten in *Parsifal*, weil er der – allerdings irrtümlichen – Annahme war, „Fal-par-si", die Silbenumstellung von Par-si-fal, habe im Arabischen die Bedeutung „reiner Tor".[10]

Wagner verstand seine Bühnenwerke nicht mehr als Opern im herkömmlichen Sinne, und um ihre Besonderheit zu kennzeichnen, versah er sie mit ungewöhnlichen Untertiteln. So heißt *Der Ring des Nibelungen* „Ein Bühnenfestspiel" und *Parsifal* „Ein Bühnenweihfestspiel". Was mit diesem Namen gemeint ist, erklärte Wagner in seinem Bericht über die erste Aufführung *Das Bühnenweihfestspiel in Bayreuth 1882*.[11] Das im Titel enthaltene Wort „Weihe" sollte freilich nicht primär religiös verstanden werden, sondern zielt vielmehr auf den ursprünglich kultischen, zeremoniell-rituellen Sinn von Theater. Daher ist es falsch, für die Ausführung der Musik prinzipiell langsame, „weihevolle" Tempi zu wählen.

Das Vorspiel wurde vorab instrumentiert, weil Wagner es seiner Frau Cosima zum Geburtstag am 25. Dezember 1878 vorspielen lassen wollte. Dazu engagierte er die Meininger

---

[1] *Richard Wagner, Sämtliche Werke*, Bd. 30, *Dokumente zur Entstehung und ersten Aufführung des Bühnenweihfestspiels Parsifal*, hg. v. Martin Geck und Egon Voss, Mainz 1970, S. 11, Dokument 1.
[2] Ebda., S. 12, Dokumente 4-5.
[3] Ebda., S. 13, Dokument 8.
[4] Ebda., S. 13-17, Dokumente 9-13.
[5] Ebda., S. 68-77.
[6] Ebda., S. 17, Dokument 16.
[7] Ebda., S. 77-87.
[8] Ebda., S. 87-134.

[9] Vgl. *Wagner-Werk-Verzeichnis*, Mainz 1986, S. 544f. (WWV 111 MUSIK II, III, VI).
[10] Vers 689-691: Dich nannt' ich, tör'ger Reiner, „Fal parsi", – Dich, reinen Toren: „Parsifal". (Verszählung nach: *Richard Wagner, Parsifal. Ein Bühnenweihfestspiel. Textbuch mit Varianten der Partitur*, hg. v. Egon Voss, Stuttgart 2005).
[11] Wagner, Sämtliche Werke (wie Anmerkung 1), S. 63-67, Dokument 241.

VII

Hofkapelle, die das Stück unter seiner Leitung in Haus Wahnfried spielte.[12] Das Manuskript dieser ersten Fassung des Vorspiels, die in der Partitur des gesamten Werks durch eine zweite Fassung ersetzt wurde, ist erhalten und erscheint in Band 21 Supplement der Ausgabe *Richard Wagner, Sämtliche Werke* erstmals im Druck. Von dort stammt auch der hier mitgeteilte Konzertschluss.

Wagner selbst erläuterte das Vorspiel durch einen Text, den er anlässlich der Aufführung des Vorspiels für Ludwig II. Bayern am 12. November 1880 verfasste:[13]

Vorspiel zu Parsifal.
Liebe – Glaube – : Hoffen?
Erstes Thema: „Liebe".
„Nehmet hin meinen Leib, nehmet hin mein Blut, um unsrer Liebe willen!"
(Verschwebend von Engelstimmen wiederholt.)
„Nehmet hin mein Blut, nehmet hin meinen Leib, auf dass ihr mein gedenkt!"
(Wiederum verschwebend wiederholt.)
Zweites Thema: „Glaube".
Verheissung der Erlösung durch den Glauben. – Fest und markig erklärt sich der Glaube, gesteigert, unerschütterlich selbst im Leiden. – Der erneuten Verheissung antwortet der Glaube, aus zartesten Höhen – wie auf dem Gefieder der weissen Taube – sich herabschwingend, immer breiter und voller die Brust, das menschliche Herz einnehmend, die Welt, die ganze Natur mit mächtigster Kraft erfüllend, – dann wieder nach dem Himmelsäther wie sanft beruhigt aufblickend. –
Da, noch einmal, aus Schauern der Einsamkeit erhebt die Klage des liebenden Mitleides: Bangen, heiliger Angstschweiss des Oelberges, göttliches Schmerzens-Leiden des Golgatha, – der Leib erbleicht, das Blut entfliesst und erglüht nun mit himmlischer

Segensgluth im Kelche, über Alles was lebt und leidet die Gnadenwonne der Erlösung durch die Liebe ausgiessend. – Auf ihn, der – furchtbare Reue im Herzen – in den göttlich strafenden Anblick des erglühenden Grales sich versenken musste, auf Amfortas, den sündigen Hüter des Heiligthumes, sind wir vorbereitet: wird seinem nagenden Seelenleiden Erlösung werden? – Noch einmal vernehmen wir die Verheissung, und – hoffen!

„Liebe – Glaube – Hoffen" ist selbstverständlich eine Anspielung auf den *1. Korintherbrief* des Paulus aus dem *Neuen Testament*, wo es in Kapitel 13, Vers 13 heißt: „Nun aber bleibt Glaube, Hoffnung, Liebe, diese drei; aber die Liebe ist die größte unter ihnen".

Das Vorspiel ist, was die musikalische Thematik anbelangt, kein Spiegel der gesamten Handlung. Es vermittelt allein die Welt des Grales. Zu Beginn erklingt die Melodie zu „Nehmet hin meinen Leib..." (As-Dur), die zu „Nehmet hin mein Blut...", versetzt nach c-Moll, wiederholt wird. Dem „Liebesmahl-Spruch", wie Hans von Wolzogen, Wagners Adlatus, das Thema genannt hat,[14] folgt in Takt 39 das „Gralmotiv",[15] mit dem Wagner das sogenannte Dresdner Amen zitiert, das er zuvor bereits im *Liebesverbot* und im *Tannhäuser* zur Kennzeichnung der katholisch-kirchlichen Sphäre verwendet hatte. Hier allerdings übernahm er die Fassung, die Felix Mendelssohn Bartholdy dem Thema in seiner fünften Sinfonie, der sogenannten Reformationssinfonie, gegeben hatte. Diese Sinfonie hatte Wagner am 8. Februar 1876 in Bayreuth gehört.[16] Möglicherweise war er der Meinung, Mendelssohn, vor dem er, allem Antisemitismus zum Trotz, großen Respekt hatte, habe die authentische Fassung verwendet.

In Takt 44 kommt als drittes Thema das „Glaubenthema"[17] hinzu. Weitere Thematik wird

[12] *Cosima Wagner, Die Tagebücher*, hg. v. Martin Gregor Dellin und Dietrich Mack, München/Zürich 1977, Bd. 2, S. 270f.
[13] *König Ludwig II. und Richard Wagner. Briefwechsel*, bearbeitet von Otto Strobel, Karlsruhe 1936, Bd. III, S. 186f.
[14] *Hans von Wolzogen, Thematischer Leitfaden durch die Musik des Parsifal*, Leipzig o. J., S. 17.
[15] Ebda., S. 18.
[16] *Cosima Wagner, Tagebücher* (wie Anmerkung 12), S. 969.
[17] *Wolzogen, Leitfaden* (wie Anmerkung 14), S. 19.

nicht exponiert, vielmehr bestreitet Wagner das gesamte Vorspiel mit den drei genannten Themen und daraus abgeleiteten Motiven. Das heißt, dass die Gegenwelt zum Gral, der Zauberer Klingsor mit seinen erotischen Blumenmädchen und die Verführerin Kundry musikalisch ausgeklammert bleiben. Das Vorspiel enthält nichts von den dramatischen Konflikten der Handlung.

Der Anfang des Vorspiels stellt die Ausführenden vor ein Problem. Traditionell spielen die Streichinstrumente in den Takten 1-36 (Kontrabässe ausgenommen) mit Dämpfer. Dafür gibt es jedoch keinen unmittelbaren Beleg, nicht in Wagners eigenen Niederschriften, nicht in der Bayreuther Aufführungspartitur von 1882 und nicht im Erstdruck des Vorspiels. Erst in der nach Wagners Tod erschienenen Partiturausgabe des gesamten Werks taucht die Anweisung auf. Wahrscheinlich geht sie auf einen Vorschlag des *Parsifal*-Dirigent Hermann Levi zurück, dem Wagner zugestimmt haben soll. Genaueres lässt sich dazu nicht sagen. Möglicherweise aber liegt ein Missverständnis zugrunde; denn Auslöser für Levis Vorschlag war vermutlich Folgendes: Die Takte 6-19 und 25-38 des Vorspiels entsprechen den Takten 1445-1458 bzw. 1464-1469 der Gralsszene im 1. Akt. Dort sind Dämpfer vorgeschrieben, im Vorspiel dagegen nicht, weshalb Levi wahrscheinlich für eine Angleichung plädiert hat, die Wagner zugestanden haben könnte. Die Ausdehnung der Dämpfervorschrift auf die Takte 1-6 und 20-25 wäre dann – möglicherweise – als Irrtum zu werten.[18]

Der Notentext folgt der Edition Eulenburg No. 8058, für die die Ausgabe *Richard Wagner, Sämtliche Werke*, Bd. 14, I, *Parsifal* WWV 111, hg. v. Egon Voss und Martin Geck, Mainz 1972, revidiert wurde. Der zugehörige Kritische Bericht findet sich in Bd. 14, III, Mainz 1973, S. 157ff.

Egon Voss

[18] Vgl. zu diesem Thema: *Stephan Mösch, Weihe, Werkstatt, Wirklichkeit. „Parsifal" in Bayreuth 1882-1933*, Kassel 2009, S. 147, 238. – *Egon Voss, Parsifal-Probleme. Besonderheiten der Bayreuther Aufführungen 1882 und ihre Folgen*, in: *wagnerspectrum* 12, Heft 1/2016, S. 83-87.

PARSIFAL
Prelude

Vorspiel

Richard Wagner
(1813–1883)
WWV 111

First edition "mit Dämpfer" (con sordino), no indication in the manuscript and in the score of the first performance in 1882.
Im Erstdruck „mit Dämpfer". Diese Vorschrift fehlt sowohl im Autograph als auch in der Uraufführungspartitur von 1882.

Edited by Egon Voss
© 2019 Ernst Eulenburg Ltd, London
and Ernst Eulenburg & Co GmbH, Mainz

No. 666   EE 3765

6

9

12

Etwas zurückhaltend

*) Nach dem Erstdruck von hier an ohne Dämpfer (vgl. S.1)

4

Nach einer Bemerkung in der Uraufführungspartitur von 1882 pausierte das 1. Horn bei der ersten Aufführung in den Takten 60 bis 63.

14

5

6

20

Der Vorhang öffnet sich
vor der Bühne

Konzertschluß

Der Konzertschluß folgt der Fassung, die Wagner in der ersten Partiturniederschrift des Vorspiels gewählt hat (vgl. Dokumentenband zu Parsifal S. 9. u. 36f).